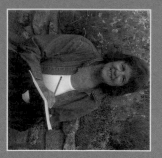

JANET WHITTLE is a professional artist and qualified teacher who specializes in flowers and landscapes in watercolour and pastel. She exhibits regularly at the Westminster Galleries in London, and has also shown her work at the prestigious Mall Galleries and other international venues. Janet has received awards from major art groups. Visit her website: www.janetwhittle.co.uk

Other books by Janet Whittle:

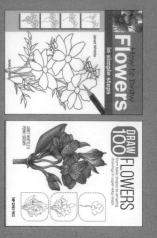

Also in the Draw 30 Series:

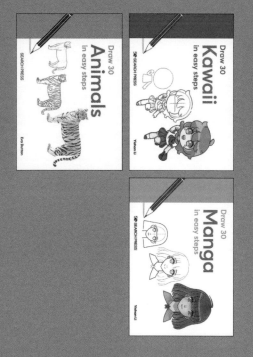

Draw 30
Flowers
in easy steps

Janet Whittle

Search Press

About this book

Each of these 30 drawings of flowers has
no more than eight simple steps: we start off
with black lines or shapes in the first steps, then
introduce a second colour in subsequent steps to
show the development of the drawing.

Follow the stages using a fairly soft pencil – HB, B or
2B – then you can remove any unwanted marks or tidy
up lines with an eraser. When you have completed the
drawing, you can start adding tones with shading,
or apply colour – I have chosen to use watercolour,
but you could use any medium.

By simply looking at flowers, we can
start to appreciate the beauty that
surrounds us.

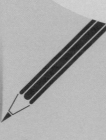

The contents

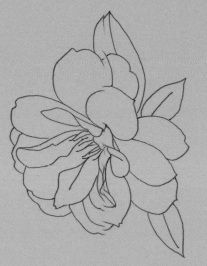

The Drawings

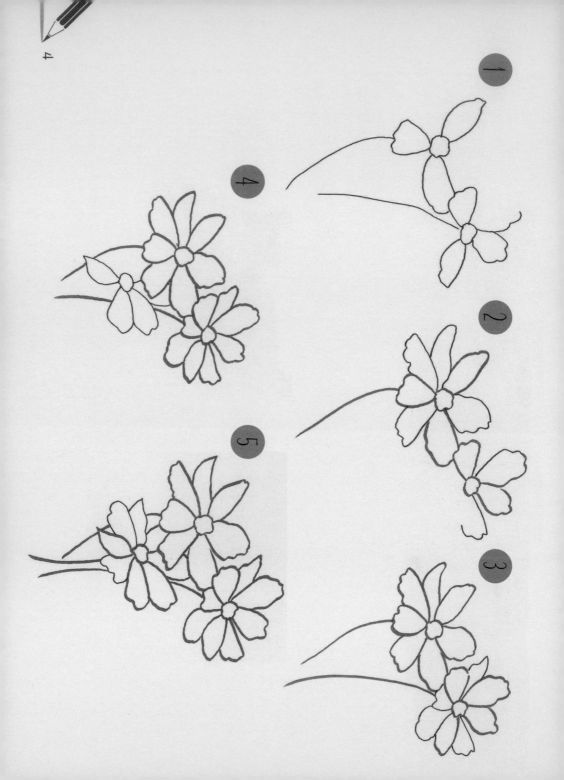

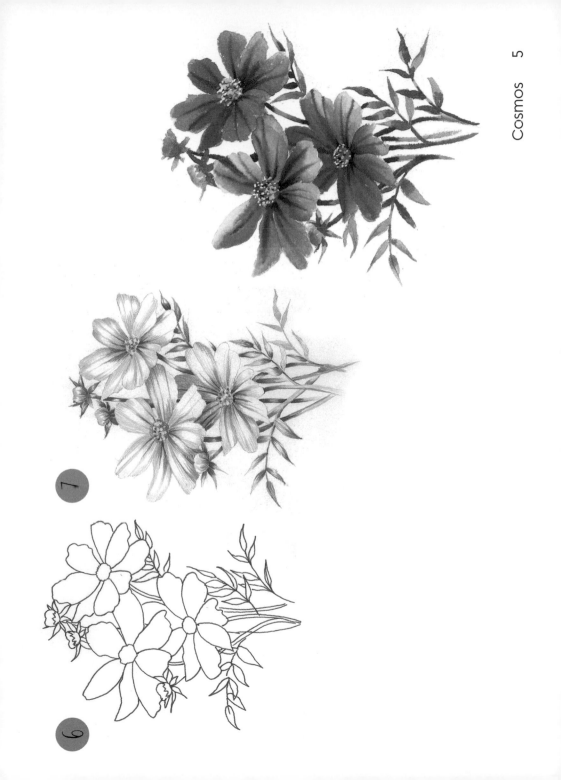

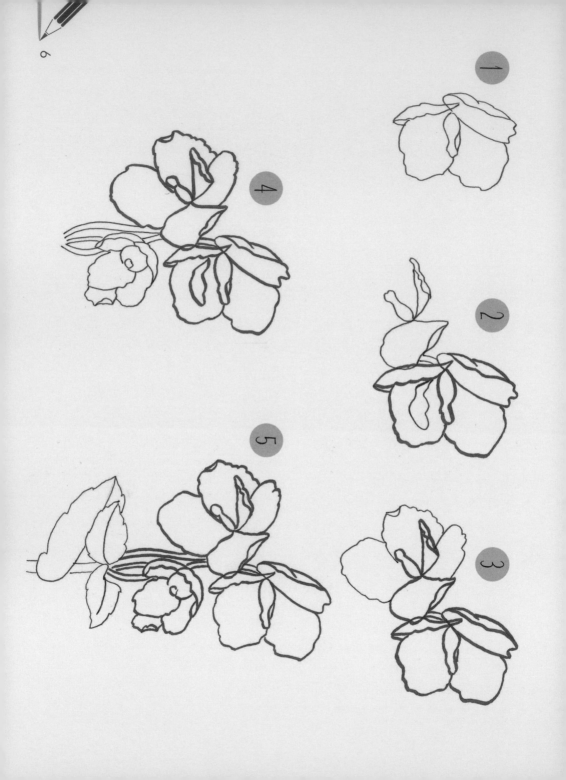

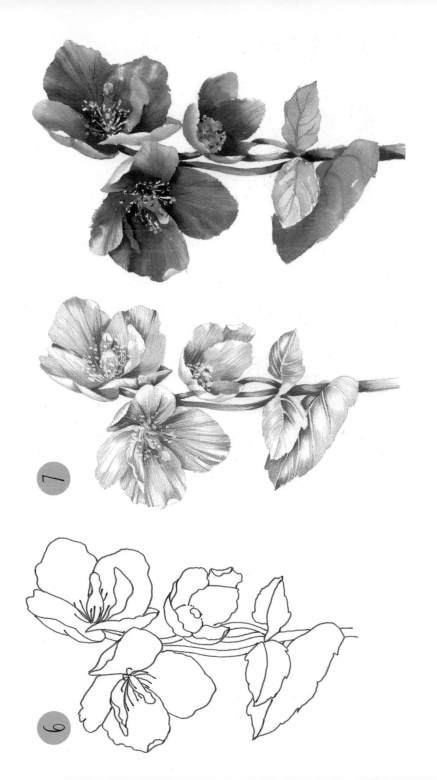

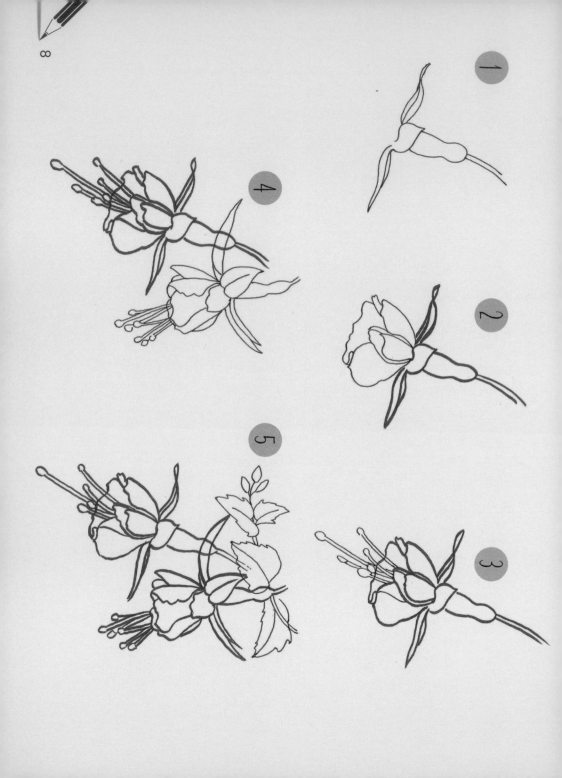

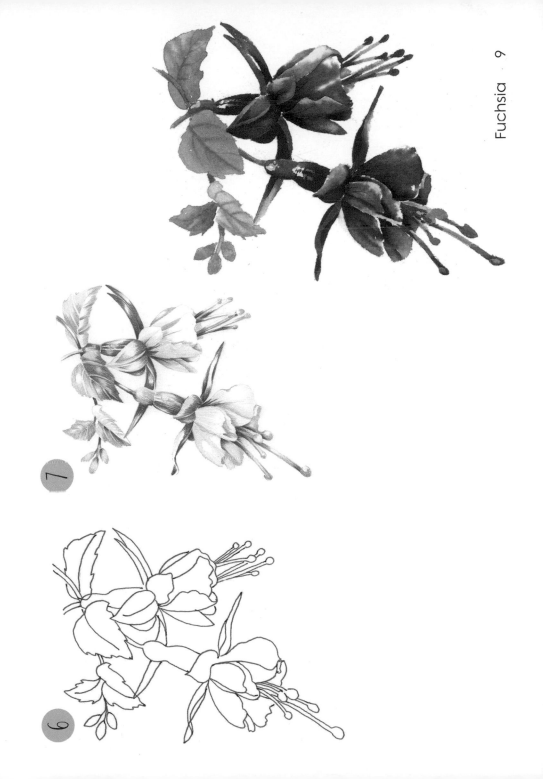

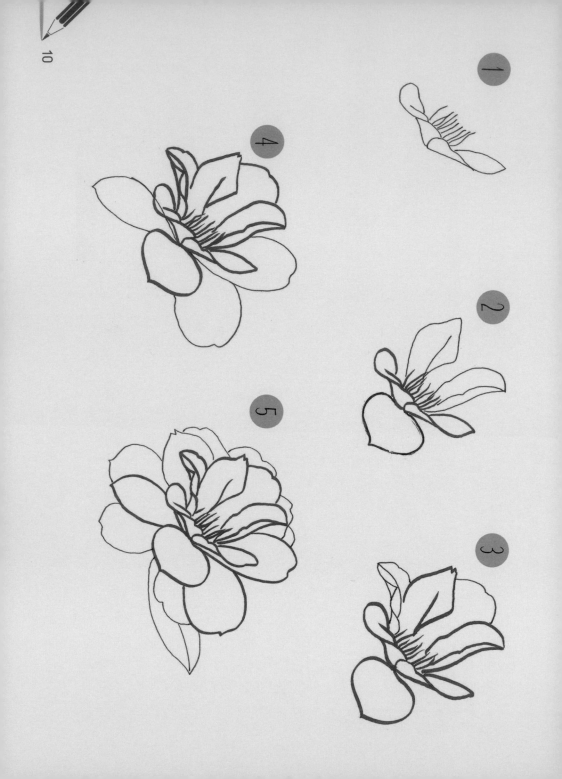

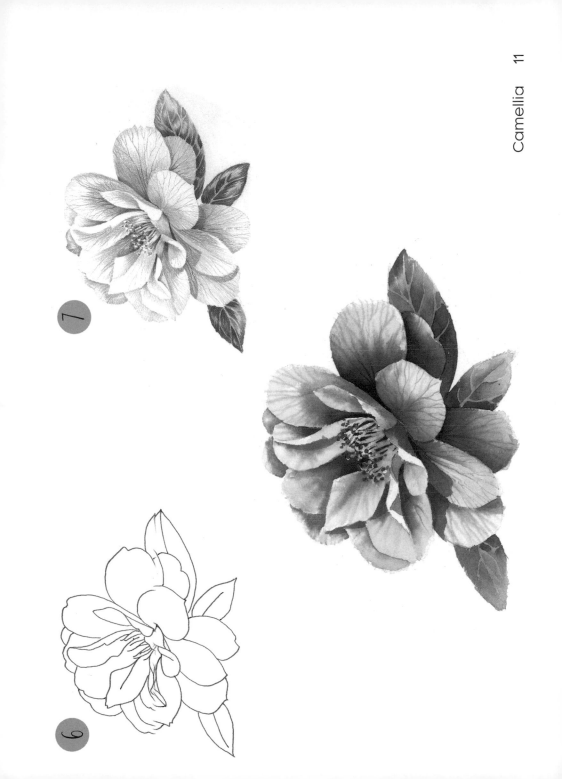

12

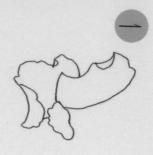

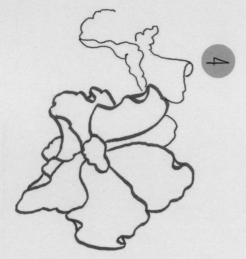

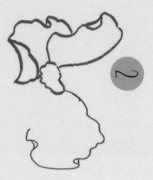

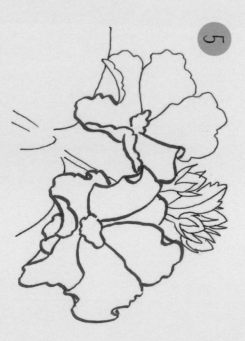

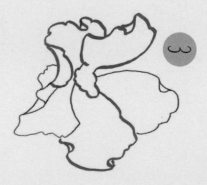

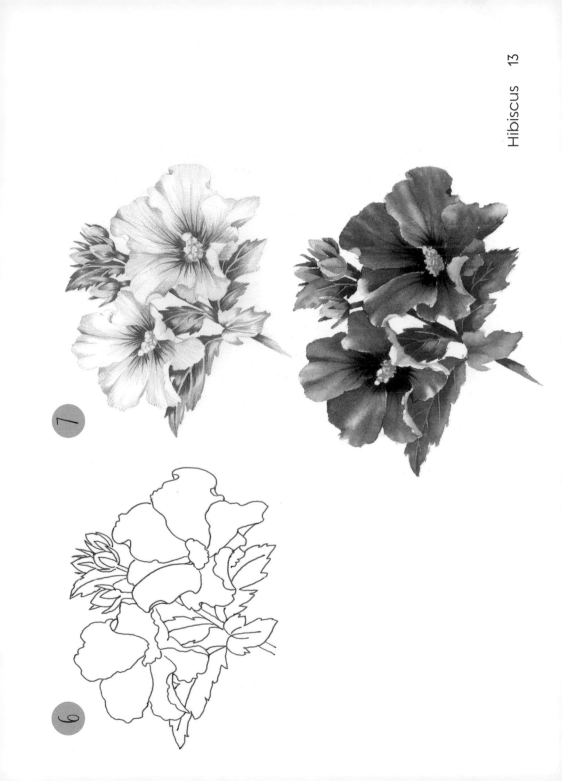

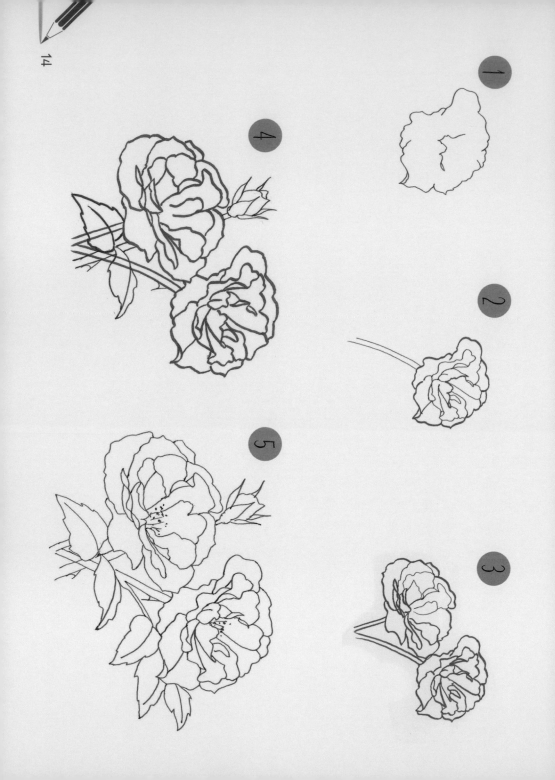

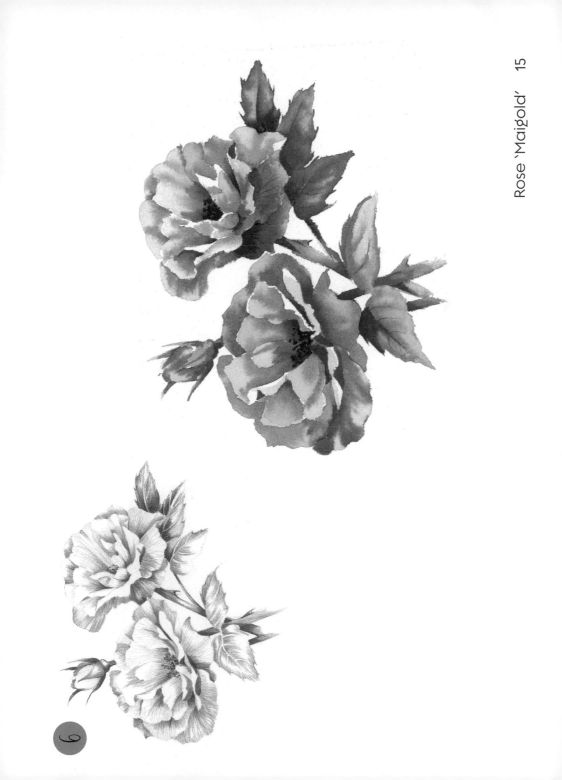

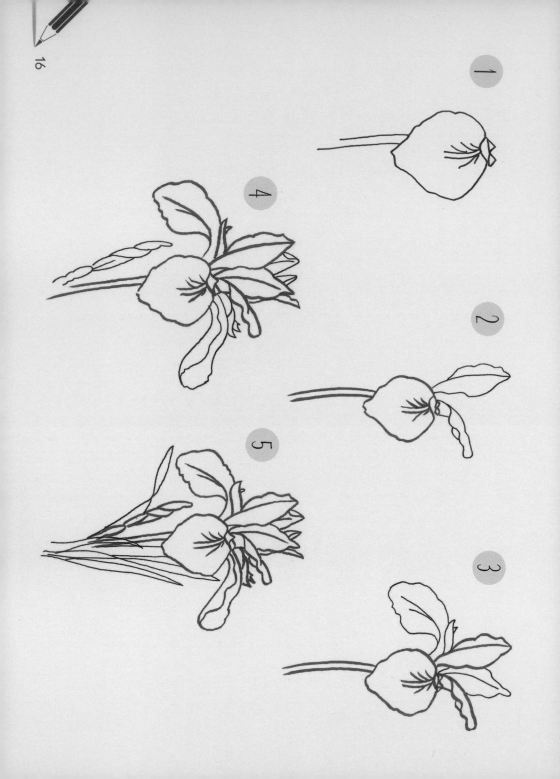

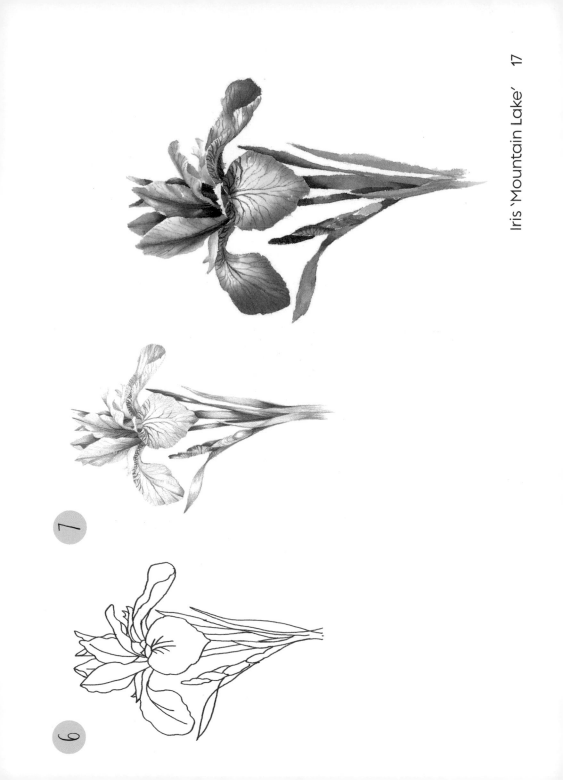

7

6

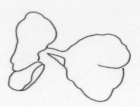

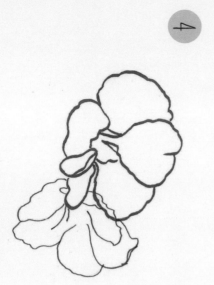

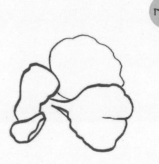

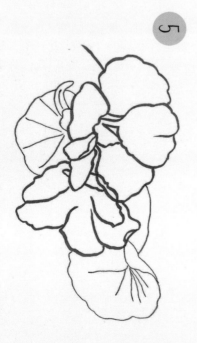

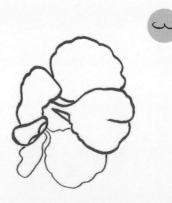

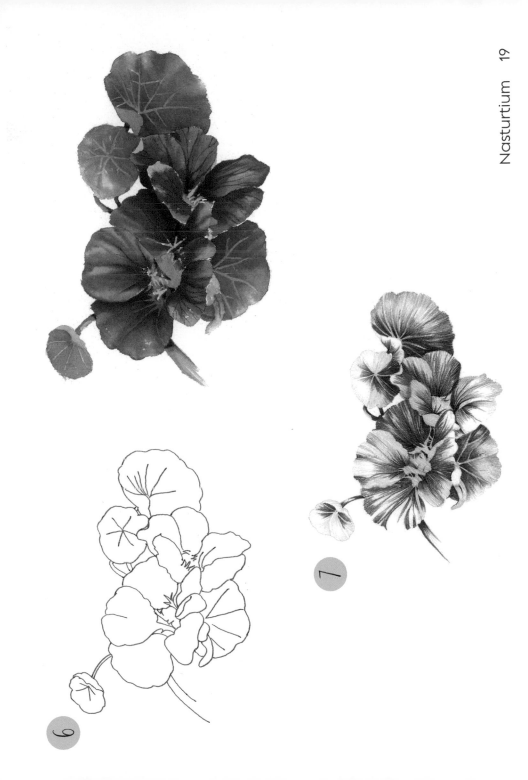

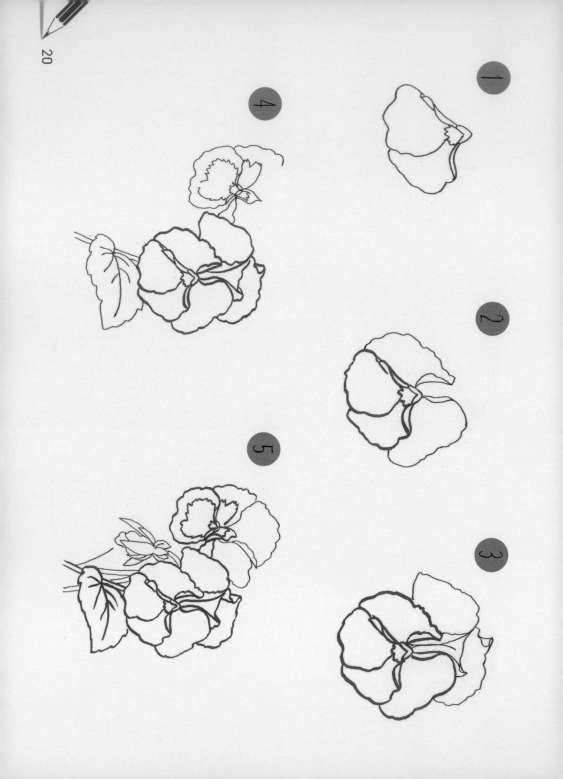

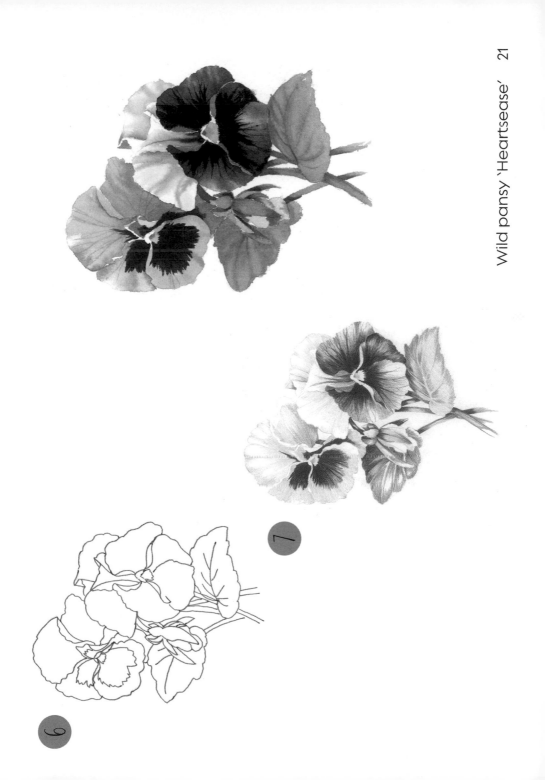

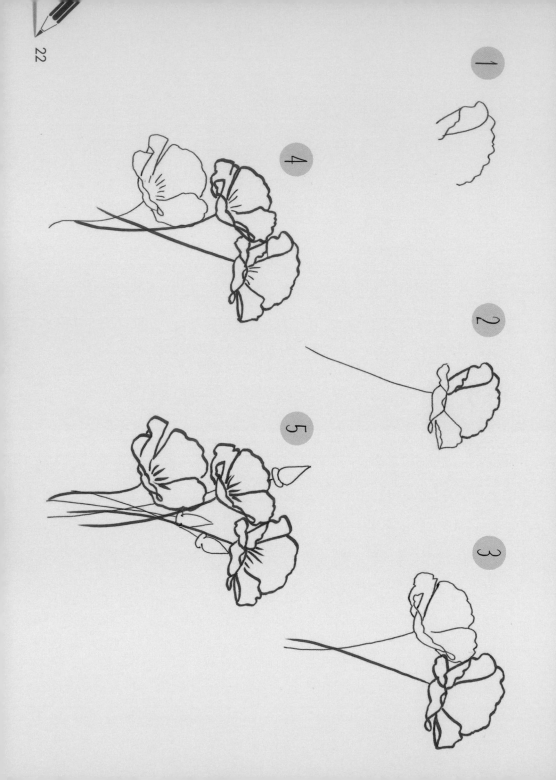

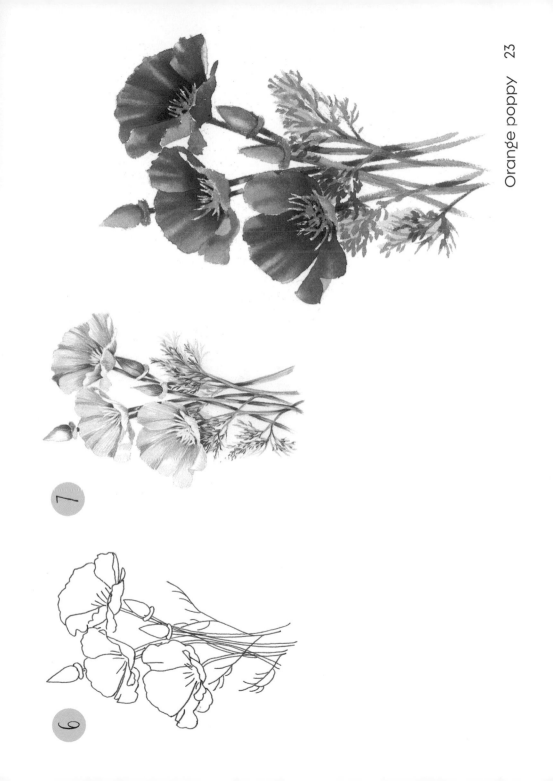

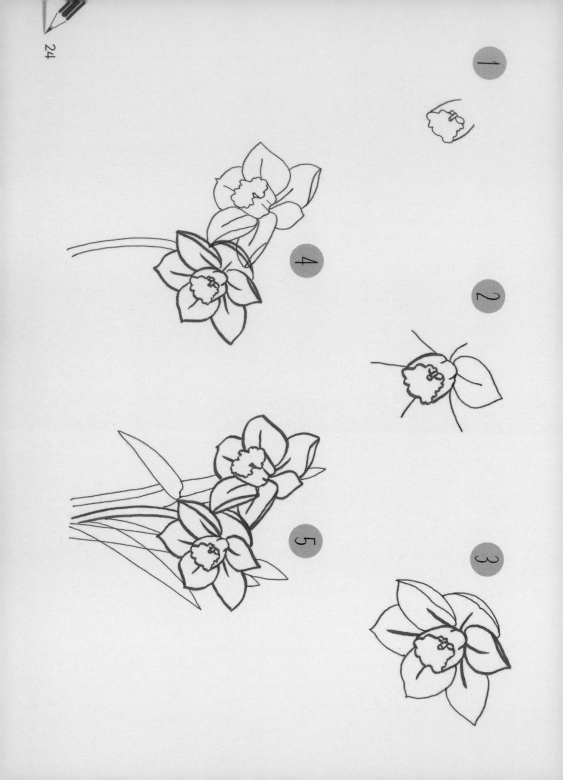

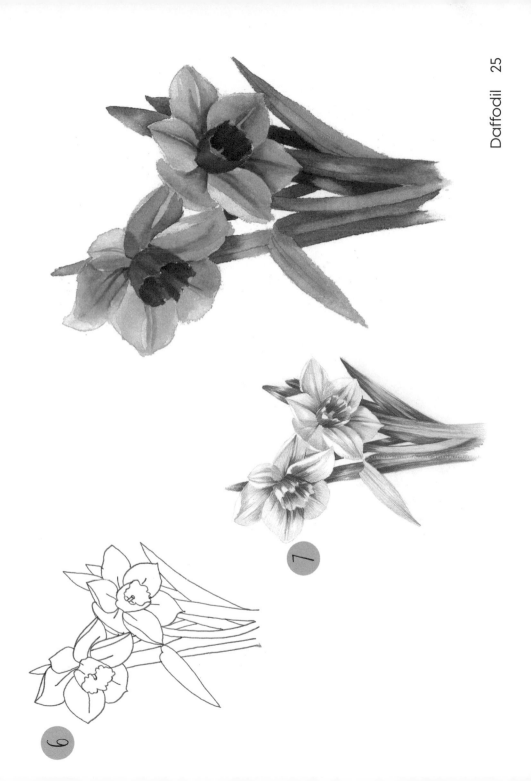

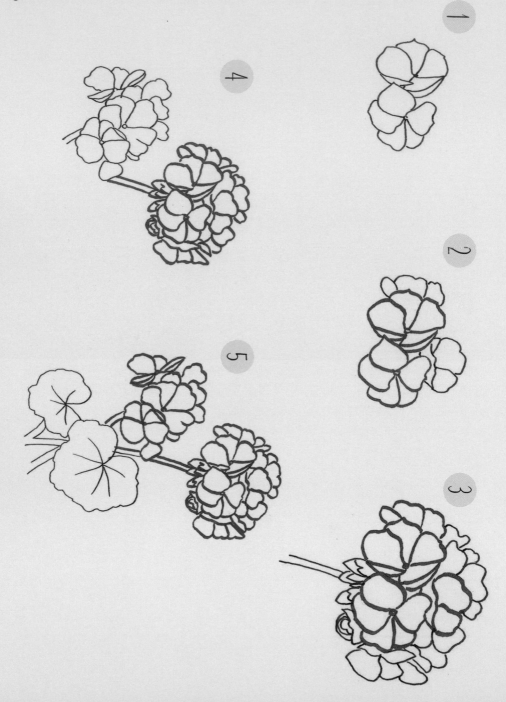

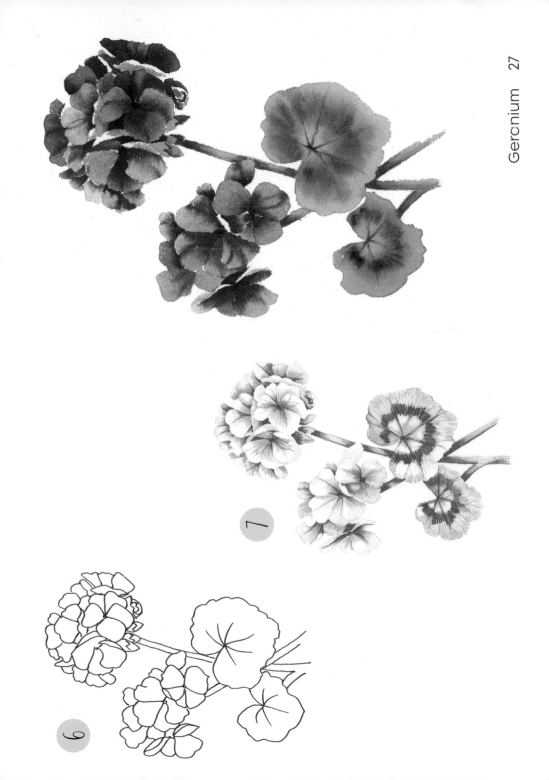

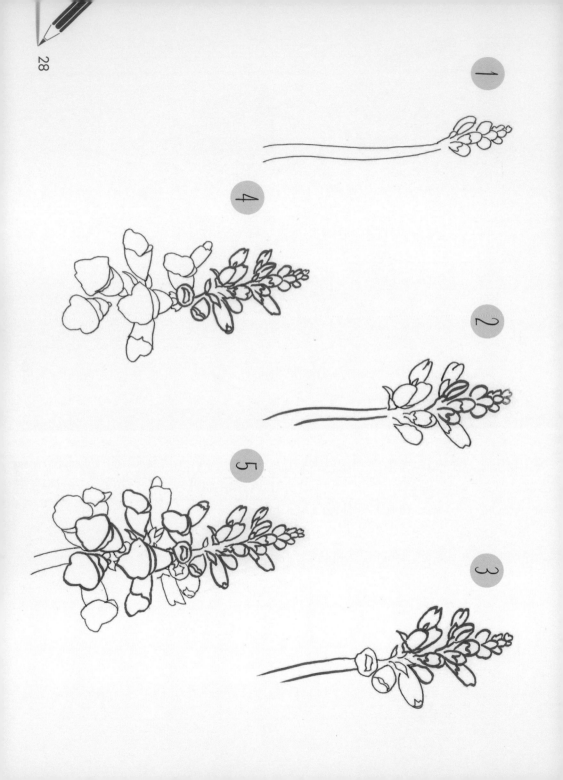

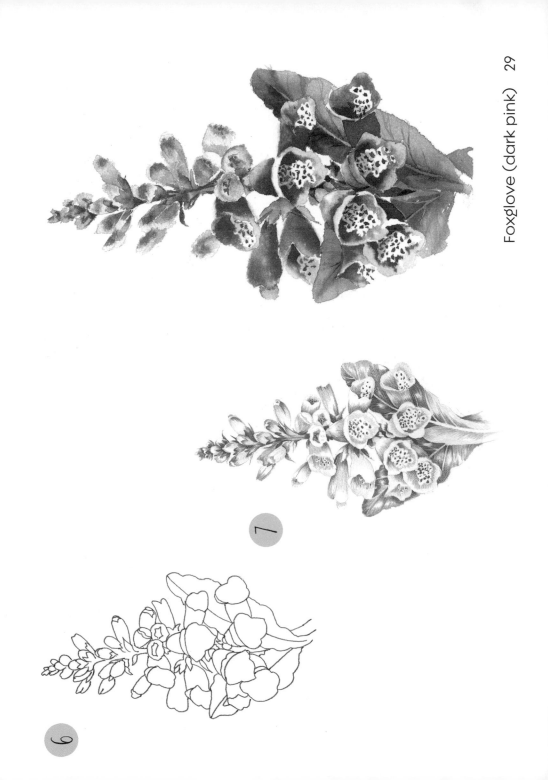

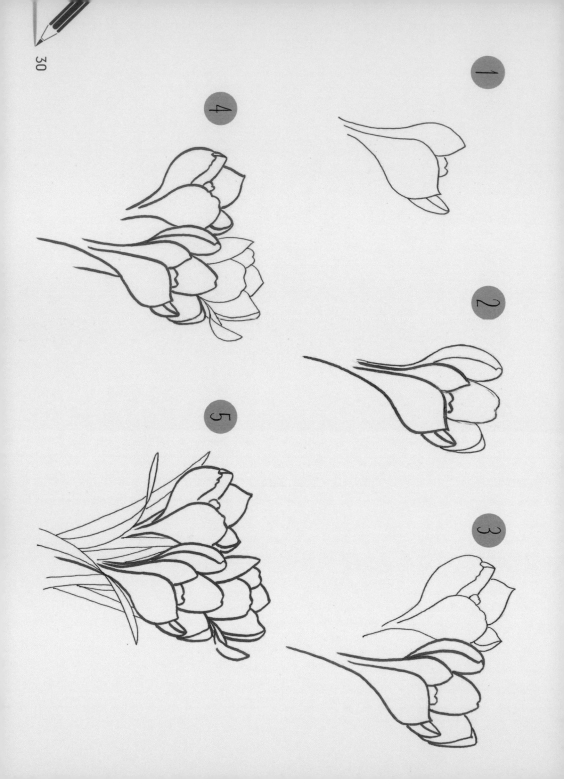

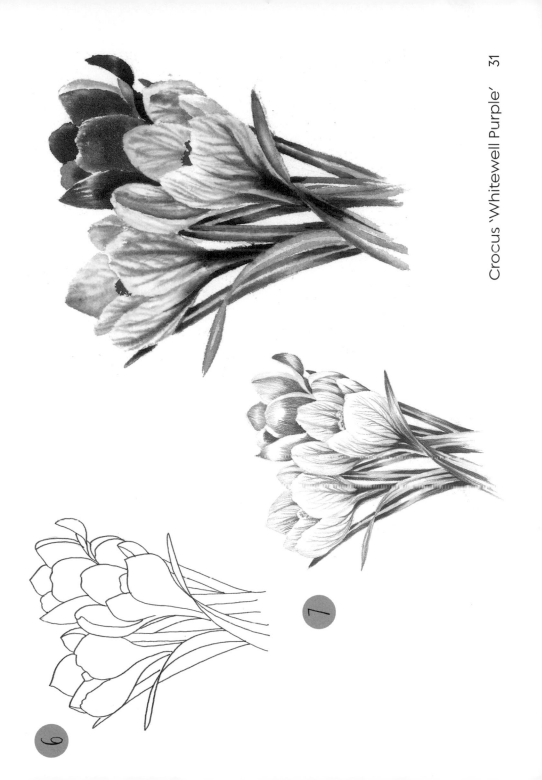

1

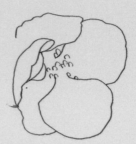

4

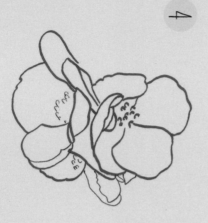

2

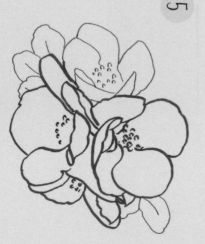

5

3

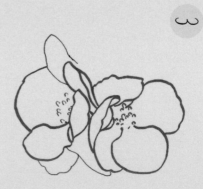

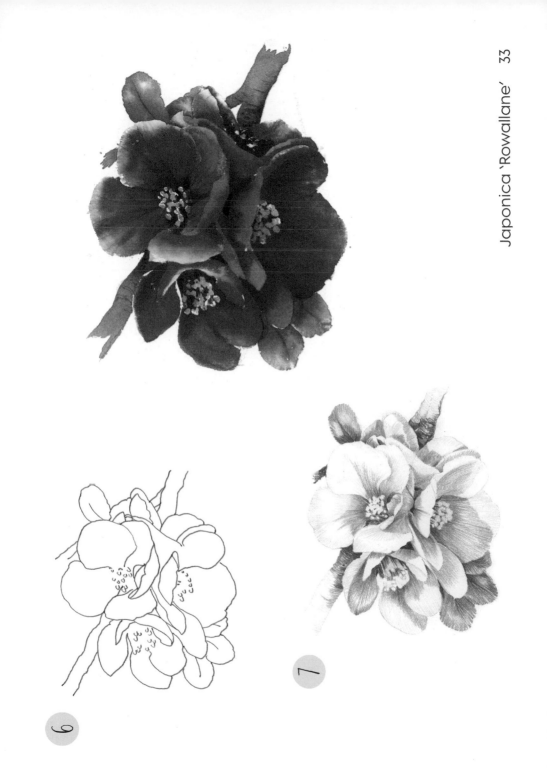

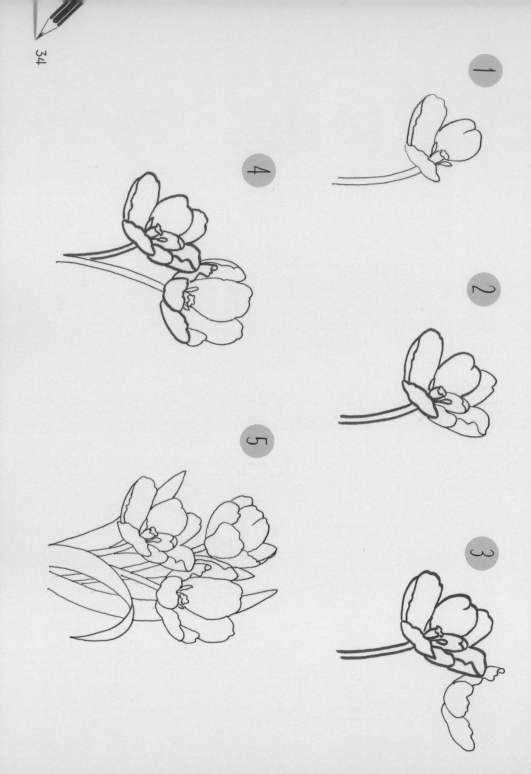

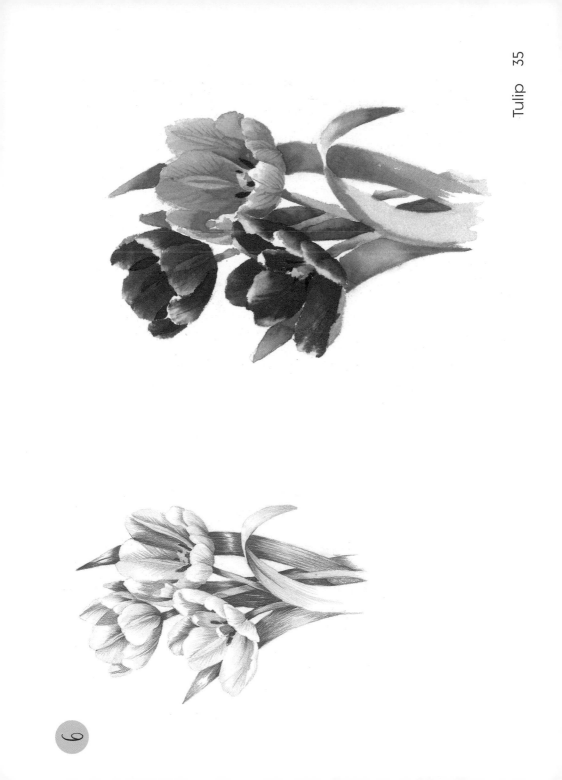

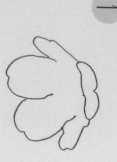

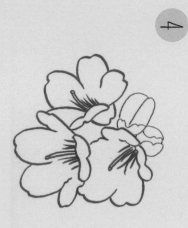

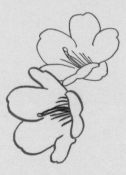

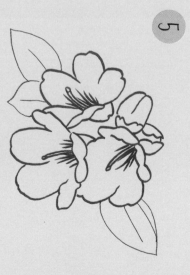

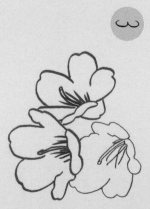

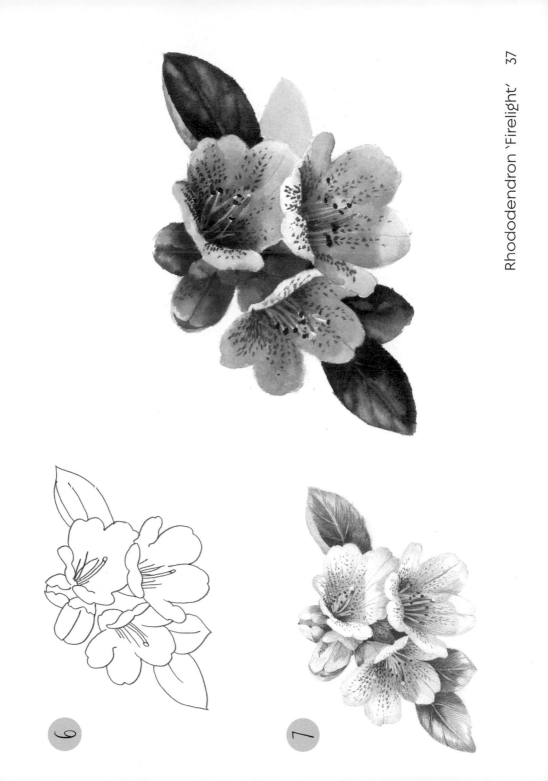

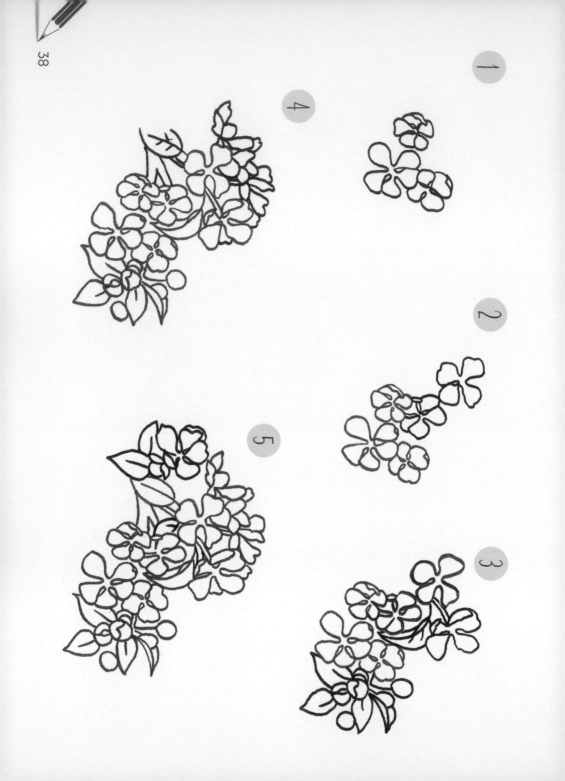

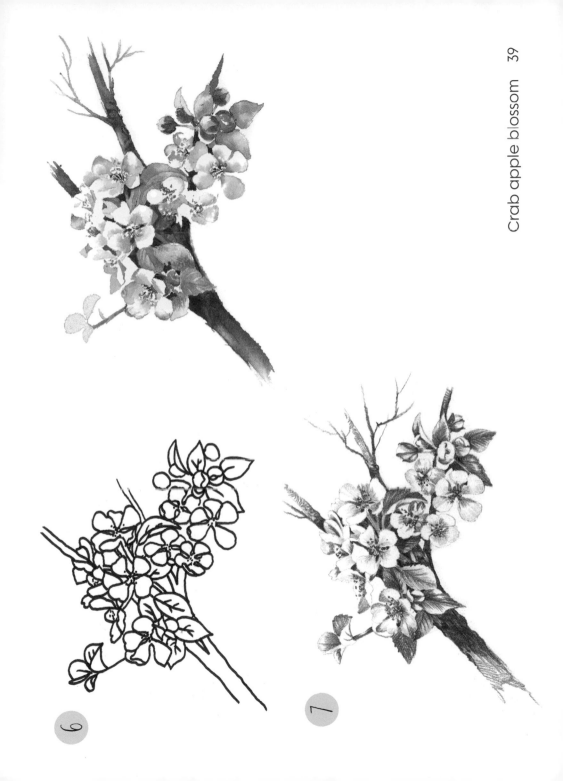

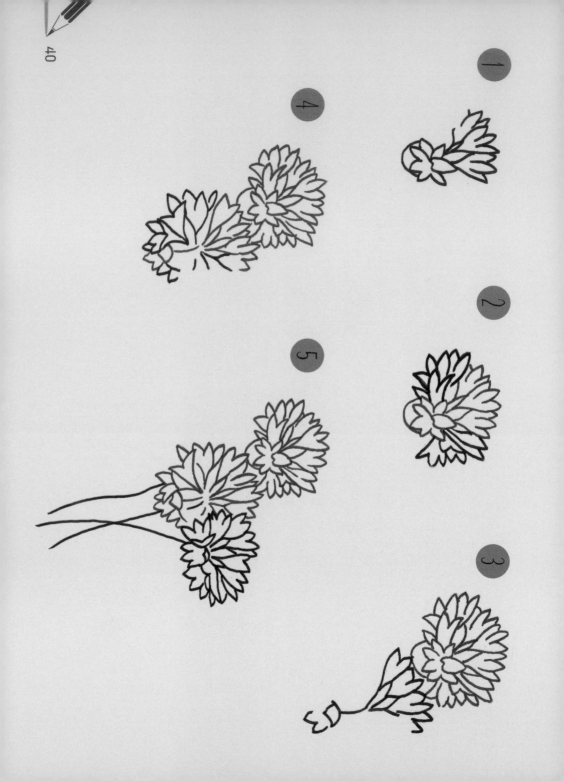

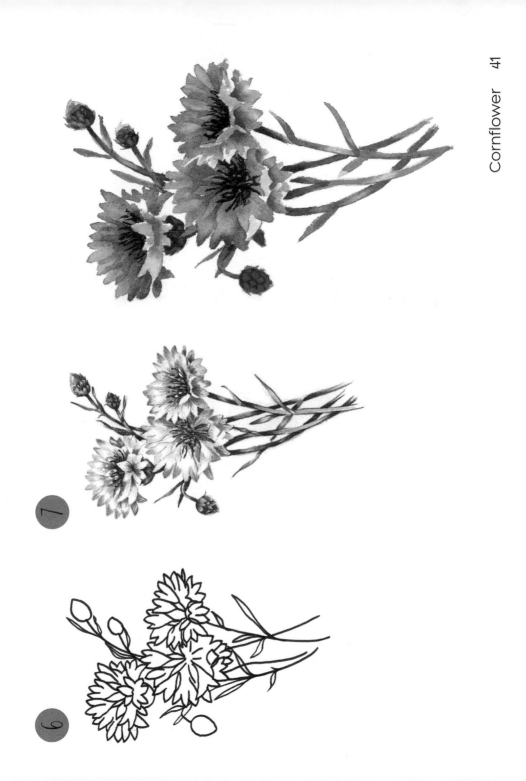

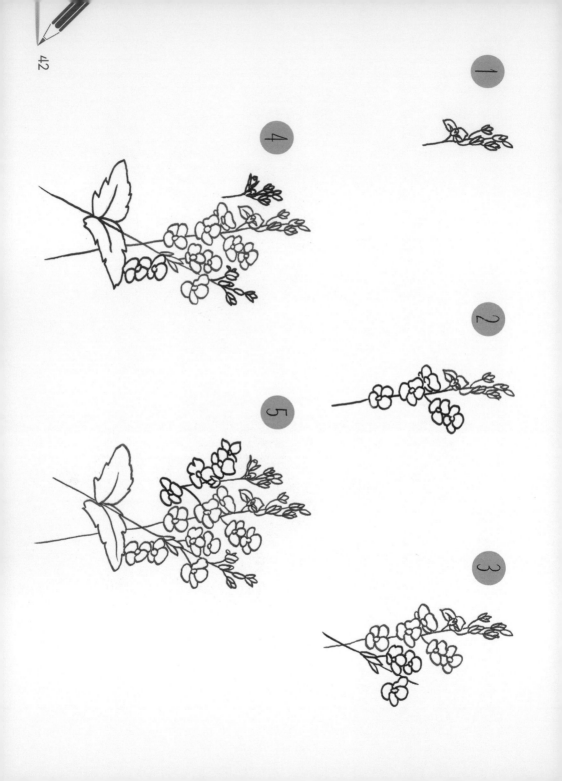

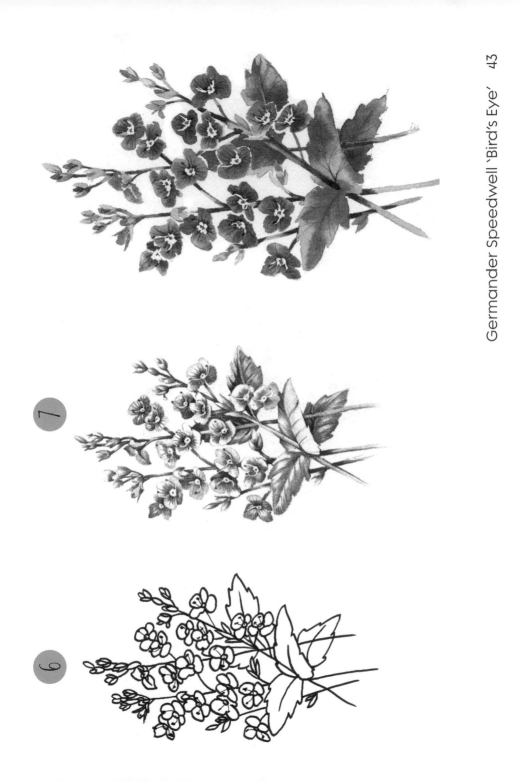

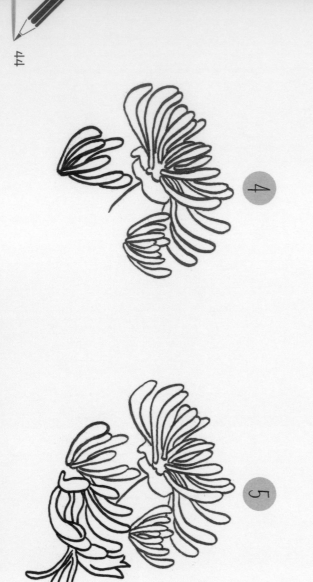

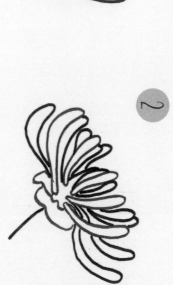

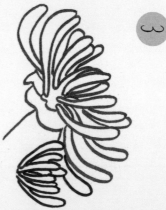

44

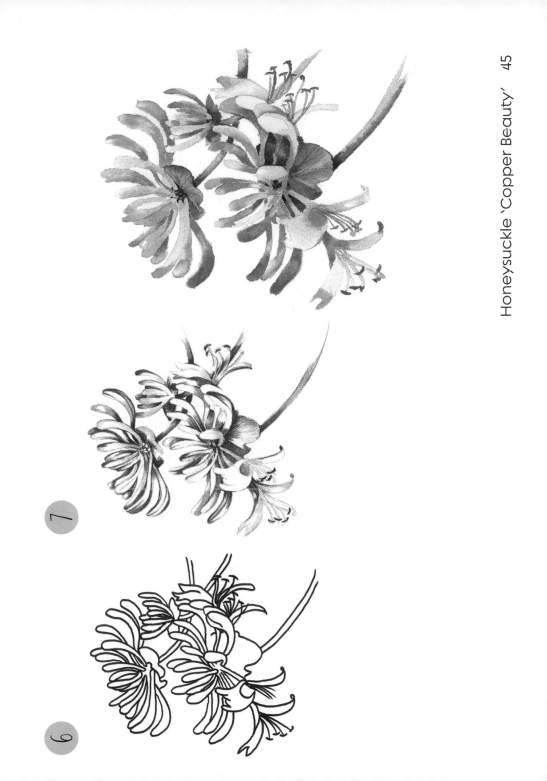

1

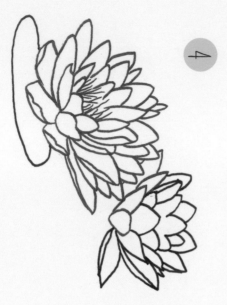

4

2

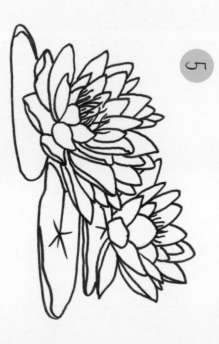

5

3

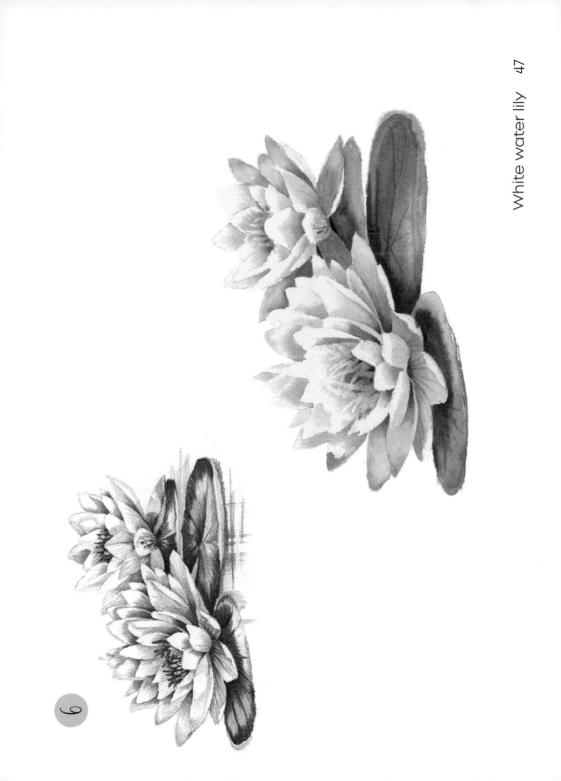

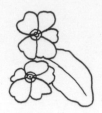

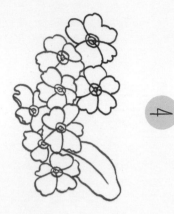

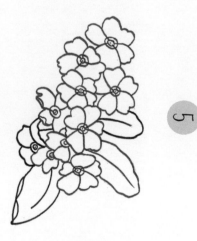

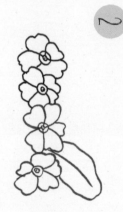

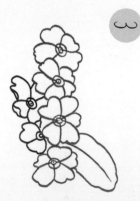

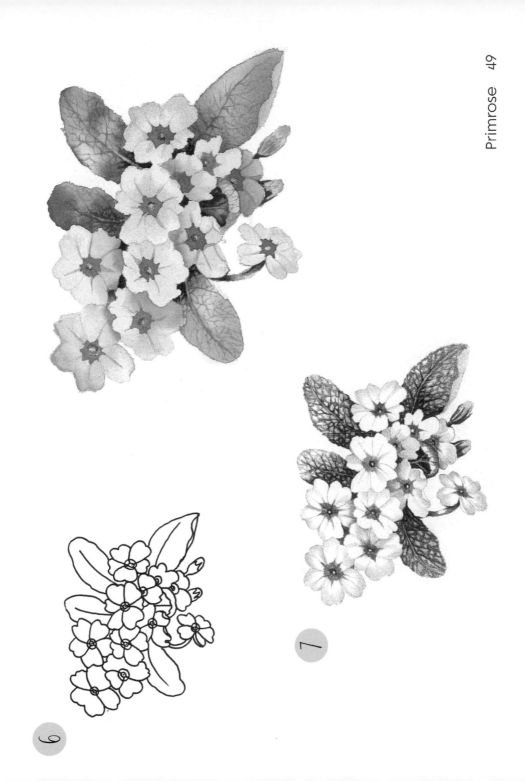

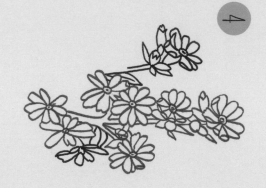

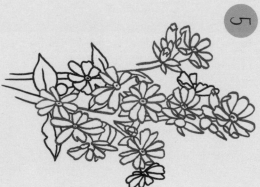

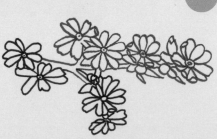

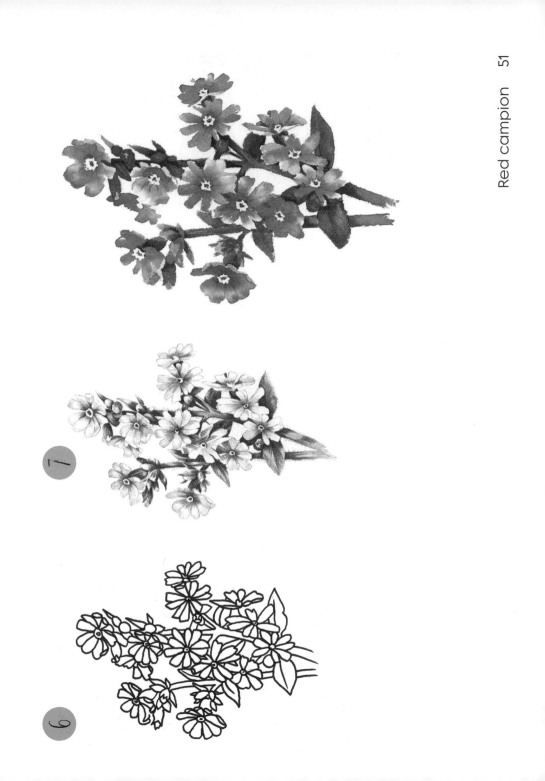

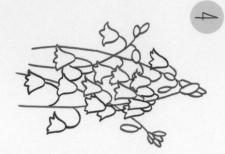

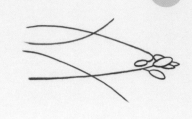

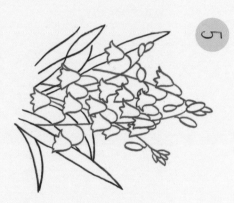

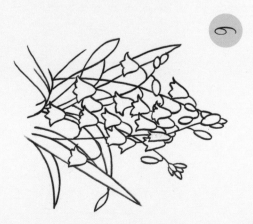

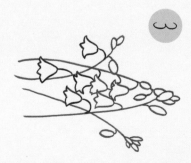

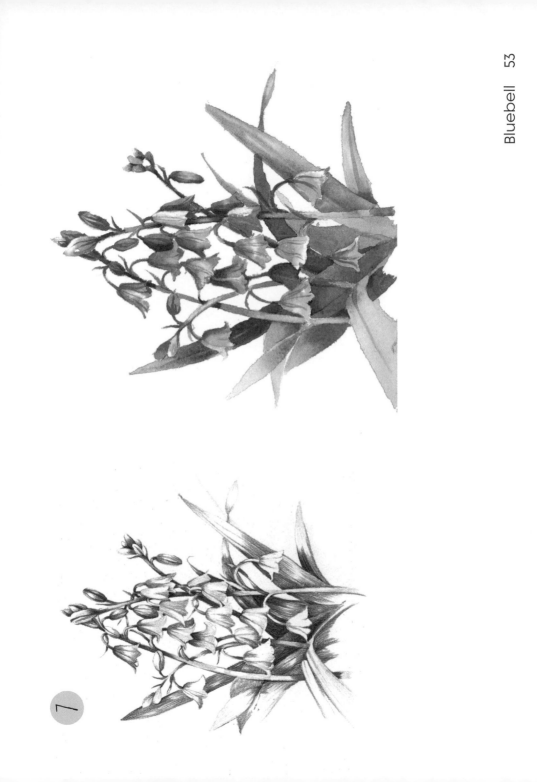

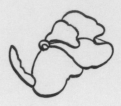

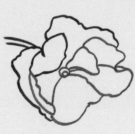

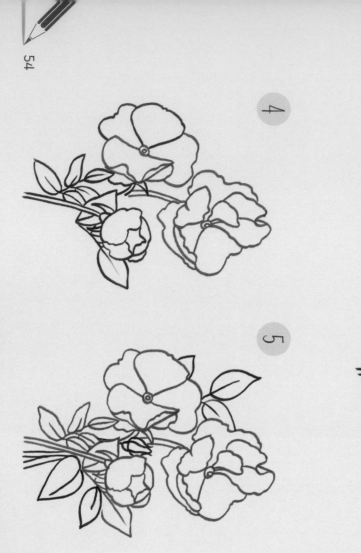

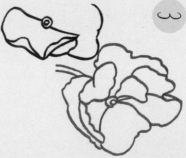

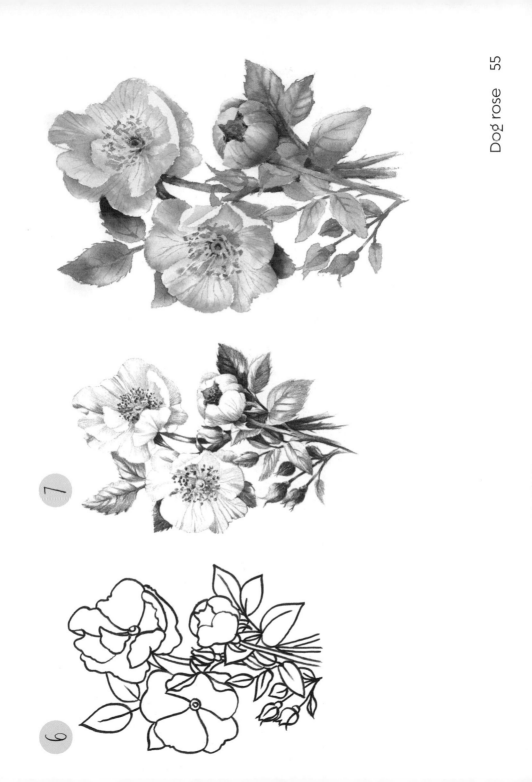

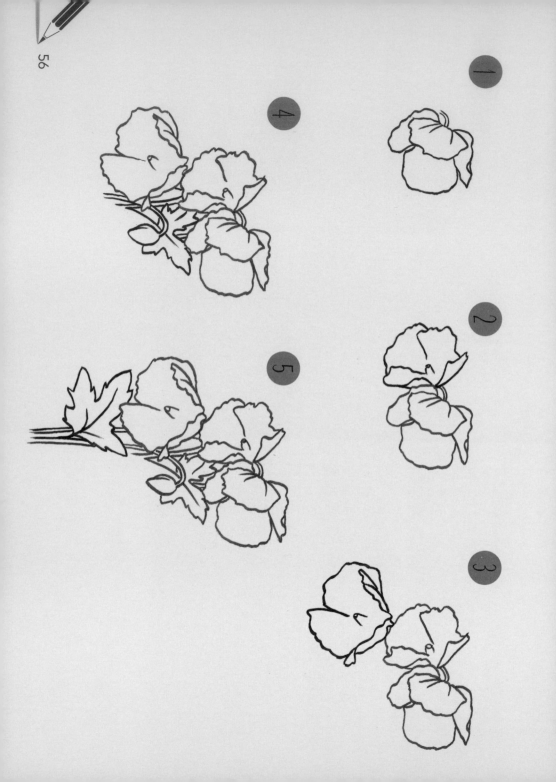

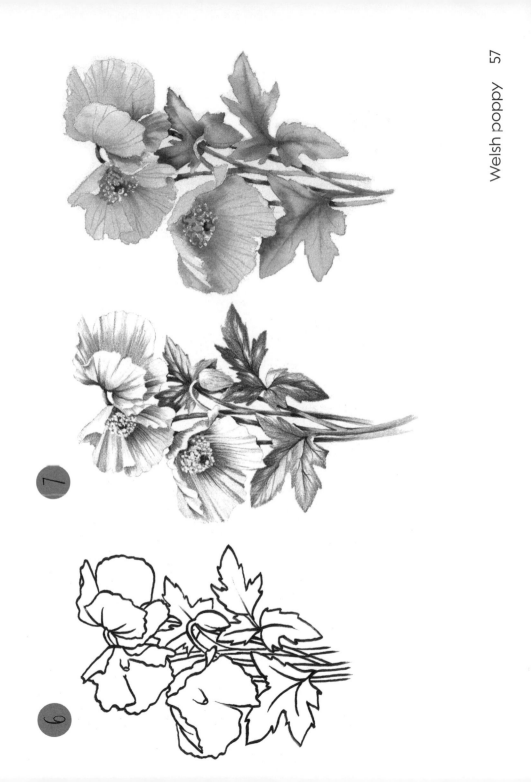

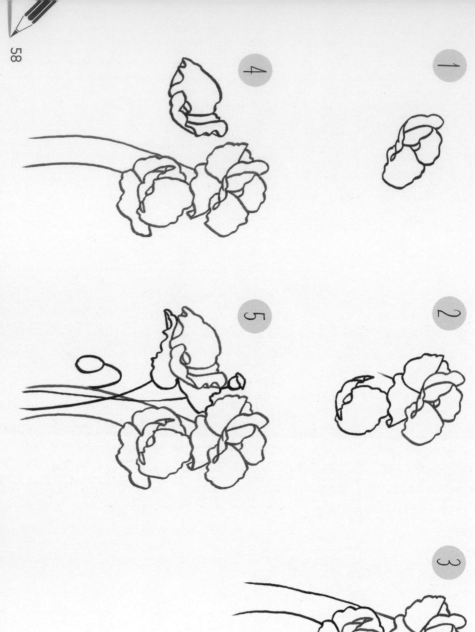

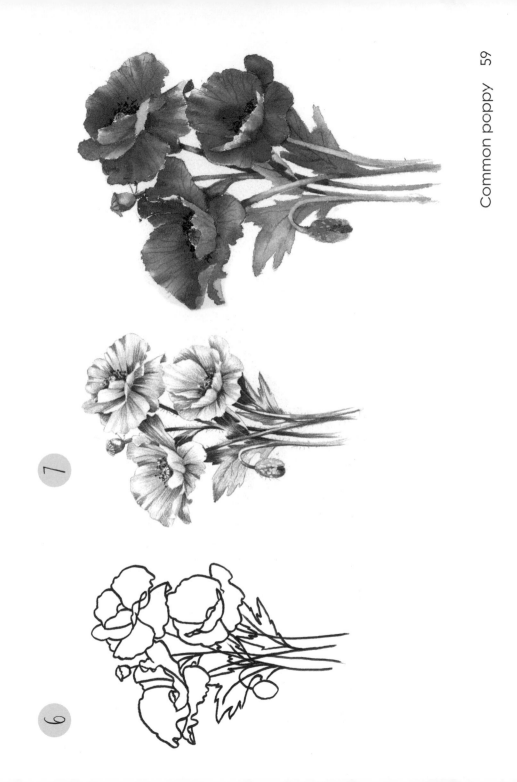

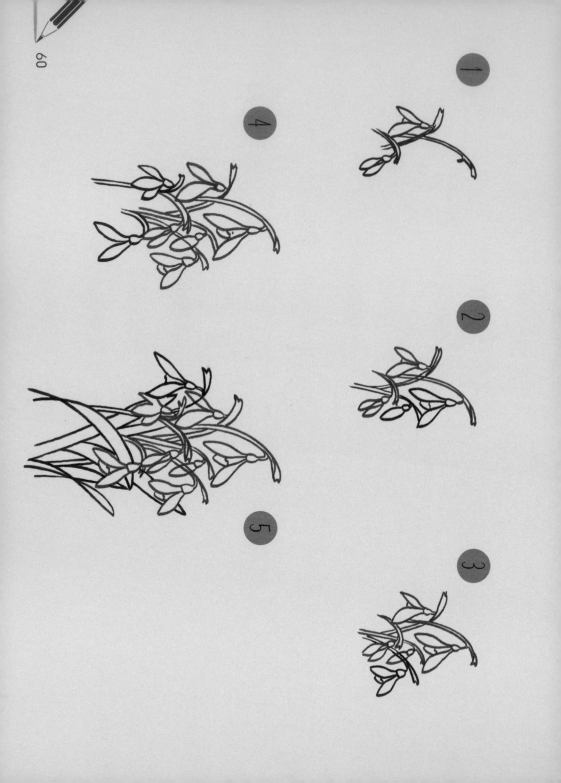

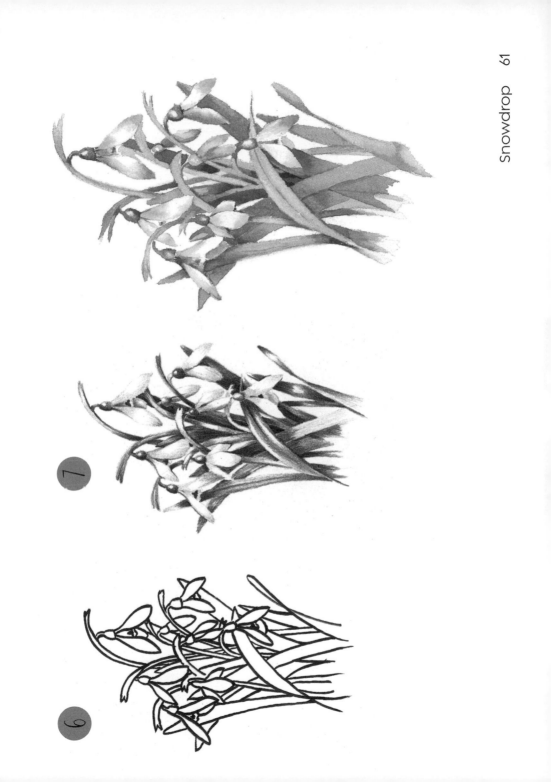

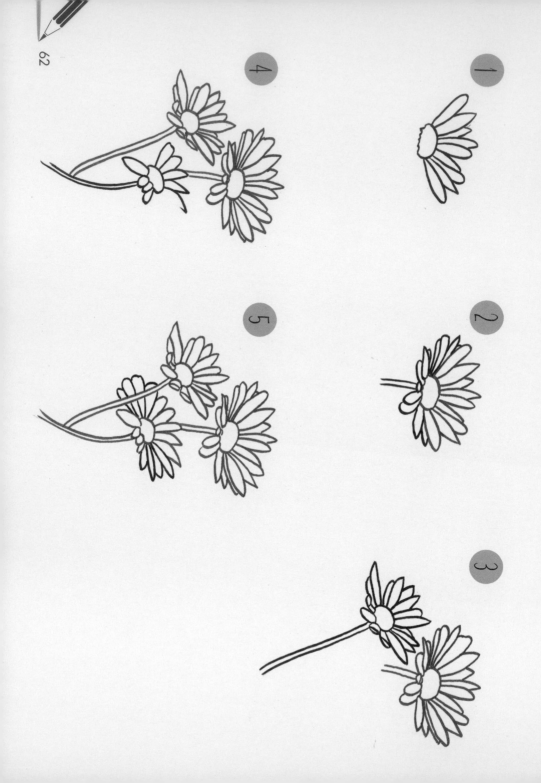

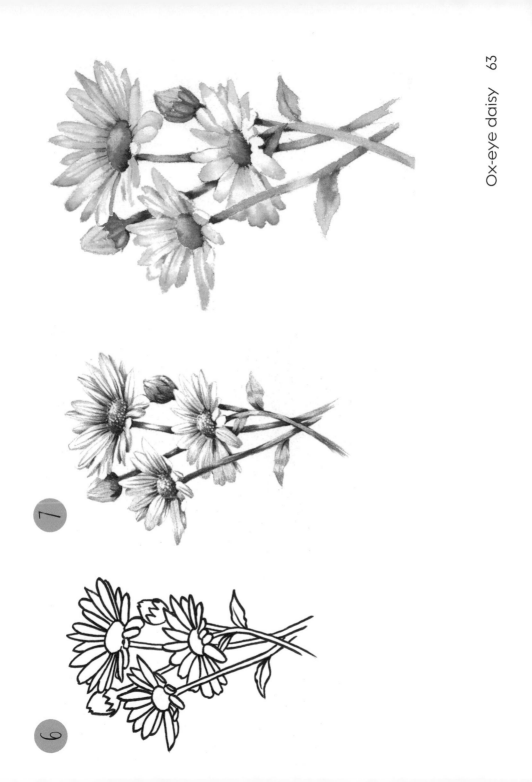

7

6

First published in 2024

This book uses material previously published in
How to Draw: Flowers – in simple steps, 2008, and
How to Draw: Wild Flowers – in simple steps, 2010

Search Press Limited
Wellwood, North Farm Road,
Tunbridge Wells, Kent TN2 3DR

ISBN: 978-1-80092-187-0
ebook ISBN: 978-1-80093-167-1

For further ideas and inspiration and to join our free online
community, visit www.bookmarkedhub.com

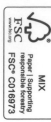

MIX
Paper | Supporting
responsible forestry
FSC® C016973

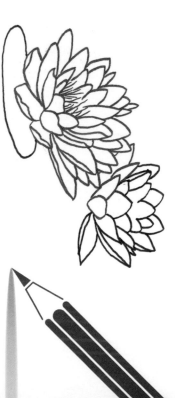

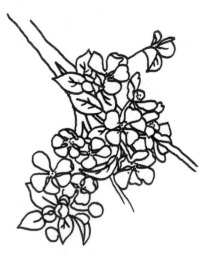